MW01378623

ISBN 979-8-9889779-1-9 (paperback)

Printed in USA

First Edition

This journal is a journey. One filled with love, growth and the kind of connection that only deepens over time. As you write, reflect, and plan together, may these pages become a place where you rediscover each other in new ways, celebrate the little moments, and embrace the beauty of your unique story. This is not just a book; it's a space for your hearts to meet, even when life gets busy.

Let this journal inspire you to be intentional in your relationship, to nurture the love you've built, and to dream boldly about the future. Whether you're recording memories, planning adventures, or expressing gratitude, each entry is a step toward strengthening the bond that keeps you together. Enjoy every moment of this beautiful journey!

MORNING CONFESSION

Today, we wake up with love in our hearts and gratitude for each other.

We embrace each challenge, knowing we face it side by side.

We choose connection over distractions.

Let patience flow between us, even in moments of stress.

We choose to communicate openly and listen with understanding.

We will listen to each other and respond with kindness.

We will embrace each other's flaws and celebrate our growth.

No matter how busy we get, we'll make time to connect.

RELATIONSHIP CHECKLIST
Where are we now?

Place an (X) in the box in your column if you do any
or all of the following.

	His	Hers
Compliment your partner	☐	☐
Listen to your favorite music together	☐	☐
Laugh Together	☐	☐
Plan a weekly date night	☐	☐
Hug, hold hands, or kiss for 10 seconds	☐	☐
Set aside time to talk without distractions	☐	☐
Send a sweet text message	☐	☐
Take a walk together	☐	☐
Spend quality time together	☐	☐

THANKFUL

Take a moment together to reflect on your journey as a couple.
Write down three things you appreciate about your partner.

HIS | HERS

> "Our marriage is a journey, and we are committed to growing and evolving together."

"Our love is a safe space where we can be our true selves."

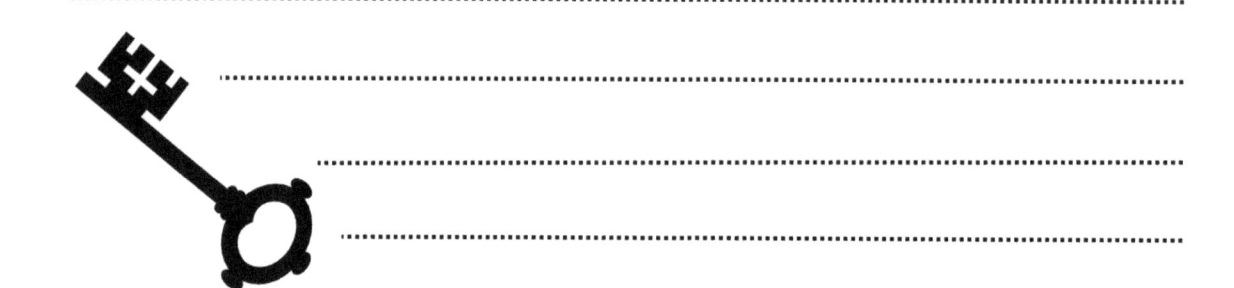

WEEKLY REFLECTION

DATE:

WHAT WAS THE HIGHLIGHT OF OUR WEEK TOGETHER?

_____

_____

DID WE FACE ANY CHALLENGES THIS WEEK?

- _____
- _____

_____

_____

_____

HOW DID WE HANDLE THEM?

- _____
- _____
- _____

_____

_____

_____

_____

"Our relationship is a beautiful journey that we embrace together."

"Our marriage is a place of love and understanding."

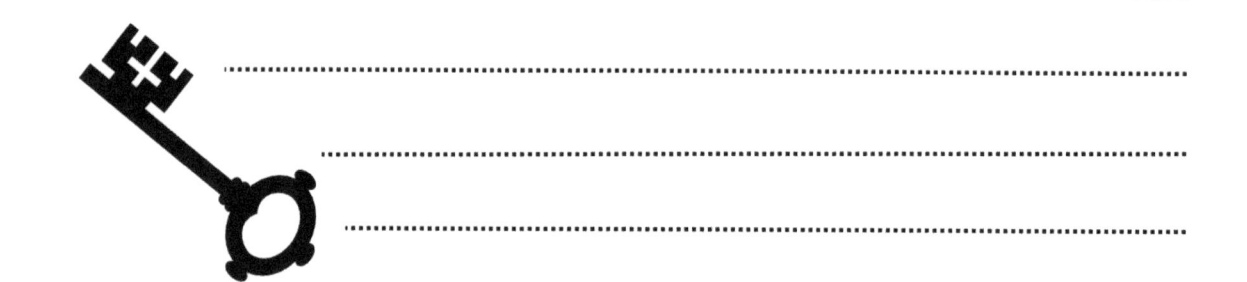

Love Letters

Write about why you fell in Love.

Love Letters

> "We trust each other completely and without hesitation."

Check-In

Today, we celebrate the love we share and the journey we are on together.

Today, this great thing happened in our relationship and we appreciate it because:

_____

_____

_____

_____

Today, this not so great thing happened to us and this is how we handled it:

_____

_____

_____

_____

Today, how did we show love to each other, even in small ways?

_____

_____

_____

_____

Today, what was a challenge we faced, and how did we handle it together?

_____

_____

_____

"We make time for each other, no matter how busy life gets."

RELATIONSHIP REFLECTION

What worries you most about our relationship?

_____
_____
_____
_____
_____

What does love mean to you?

_____
_____
_____
_____
_____

What are some qualities we admire most in each other?

_____
_____
_____
_____
_____

How do we handle conflict?

_____
_____
_____
_____

What can we do to improve our communication during disagreements?

_____
_____
_____
_____

"We encourage each other to grow and evolve."

WEEKLY REFLECTION

DATE:

DID WE HAVE ANY MISCOMMUNICATIONS OR DISAGREEMENTS?

-
-
-

HOW DID WE HANDLE THEM?

-
-
-

WHAT CAN WE DO DIFFERENTLY NEXT TIME?

"Our love story is uniquely ours and full of joy."

Check-In

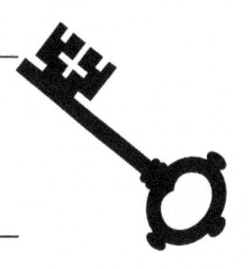

Today, we celebrate the love we share
and the journey we are on together.

Today, this great thing happened in our relationship and we appreciate it because:

_____

_____

_____

_____

Today, this not so great thing happened to us and this is how we handled it:

_____

_____

_____

_____

Today, how did we show love to each other, even in small ways?

_____

_____

_____

_____

Today, what was a challenge we faced, and how did we handle it together?

_____

_____

_____

> "We share our dreams and
> work towards them together."

RELATIONSHIP REFLECTION

In what areas do you think we need to work on trust?

_____
_____
_____
_____
_____

What do you feel is our greatest strength as a couple?

_____
_____
_____
_____
_____

How do you feel most loved and appreciated by me?

_____
_____
_____
_____

What are some goals you would like to achieve together?

_____
_____
_____
_____

How connected do you feel to one another. and what could further strengthen that bond?

_____
_____
_____
_____

> "We forgive each other quickly
> and move forward with love."

Love Letters

Share what you admire most about your partner.

Love Letters

WEEKLY REFLECTION

DATE:

DID WE HAVE ANY MISCOMMUNICATIONS OR DISAGREEMENTS?

-
-
-

HOW DID WE HANDLE THEM?

-
-
-

WHAT CAN WE DO DIFFERENTLY NEXT TIME?

"Our partnership is a blend of trust, respect, and understanding."

Growth and Improvement

WHAT DAILY HABITS COULD WE INCORPORATE TO STRENGTHEN OUR CONNECTION?

HOW CAN WE HANDLE DISAGREEMENTS MORE CALMLY?

WHAT CAN WE DO TO SHOW MORE FORGIVENESS?

HOW CAN WE BETTER SUPPORT EACH OTHER'S DREAMS?

"We will handle disagreements with grace, knowing that our connection matters more than being right."

....

....

....

....

....

....

....

....

....

....

....

....

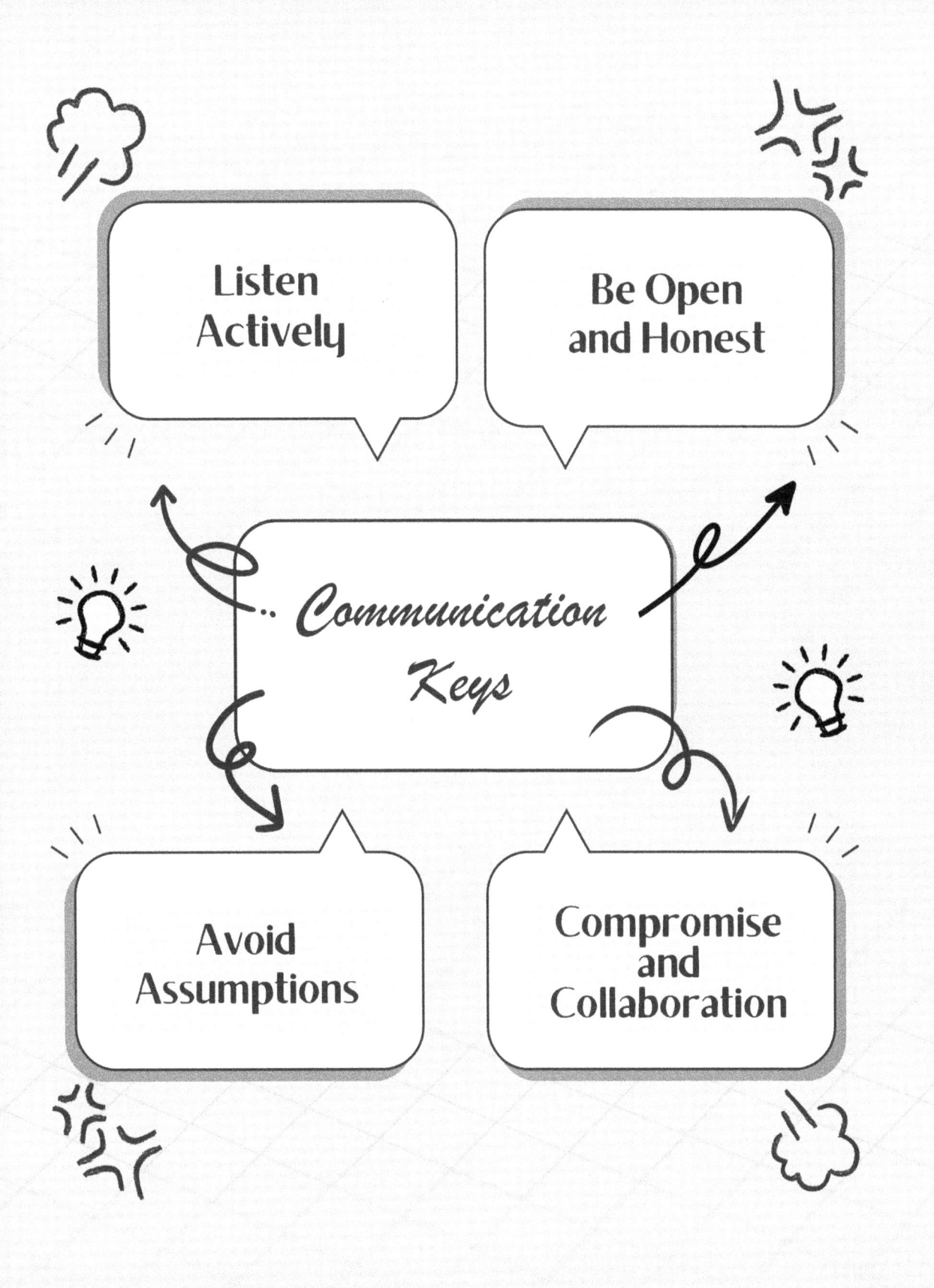

"We prioritize our relationship and nurture it daily."

WEEKLY REFLECTION

DATE:

WHAT WAS THE HIGHLIGHT OF OUR WEEK TOGETHER?

_____

_____

DID WE FACE ANY CHALLENGES THIS WEEK?

- _____
- _____

_____

_____

_____

_____

HOW DID WE HANDLE THEM?

- _____
- _____
- _____

_____

_____

_____

_____

> "We are committed to building a future filled with love and happiness."

RELATIONSHIP REFLECTION

Share a funny or unexpected memory you've experienced together?

_____
_____
_____
_____

What does a healthy and fulfilling relationship look like to us?

_____
_____
_____
_____

Was there anything that happened this week that made you feel appreciated or overlooked?

_____
_____
_____
_____

What can we do to keep our relationship exciting and spontaneous?

_____
_____
_____
_____

What is one thing I do that makes you feel supported in our relationship?

_____
_____
_____

"We communicate our needs and desires with love and respect."

WEEKLY REFLECTION

DATE:

DID WE HAVE ANY MISCOMMUNICATIONS OR DISAGREEMENTS?

-
-
-

HOW DID WE HANDLE THEM?

-
-
-

WHAT CAN WE DO DIFFERENTLY NEXT TIME?

> "Our love is a journey, and we are excited for all that lies ahead."

Check-In

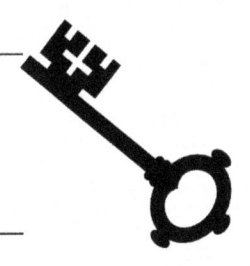

Today, we celebrate the love we share and the journey we are on together.

Today, this great thing happened in our relationship and we appreciate it because:

_____

_____

_____

_____

Today, this not so great thing happened to us and this is how we handled it:

_____

_____

_____

_____

Today, how did we show love to each other, even in small ways?

_____

_____

_____

_____

Today, what was a challenge we faced, and how did we handle it together?

_____

_____

_____

> "We embrace each other's imperfections with love and understanding."

WEEKLY REFLECTION

DATE:

WHAT WAS THE HIGHLIGHT OF OUR WEEK TOGETHER?

_____

_____

DID WE FACE ANY CHALLENGES THIS WEEK?

- _____
- _____

_____

_____

_____

HOW DID WE HANDLE THEM?

- _____
- _____
- _____

_____

_____

_____

_____

"We choose patience and compassion in our communication."

RELATIONSHIP REFLECTION

What are some habits we've developed as a couple that you appreciate?

_____
_____
_____
_____

What's a moment in our relationship that you cherish the most?

_____
_____
_____
_____

How do you feel about the way we handle financial decisions?

_____
_____
_____

What's something new you'd like to experience together?

_____
_____
_____

What are the little things we do for each other that make a
big difference in our relationship?

_____
_____
_____

"Our hearts are open to growth and change."

WEEKLY REFLECTION

DATE:

WHAT WAS THE HIGHLIGHT OF OUR WEEK TOGETHER?

_____

_____

DID WE FACE ANY CHALLENGES THIS WEEK?

- _____
- _____

_____

_____

_____

HOW DID WE HANDLE THEM?

- _____
- _____
- _____

_____

_____

_____

_____

> "We honor our commitments and keep our promises to each other."

RELATIONSHIP REFLECTION

What are some things you wish we did more often together?

_____
_____
_____
_____
_____

How can I better support your personal goals and dreams?

_____
_____
_____
_____

What are some ways we could better show appreciation for each other?

_____
_____
_____
_____

How do you feel about the way we manage household responsibilities?

_____
_____
_____

What's something you've learned from me that's impacted you positively?

_____
_____
_____
_____

> "We are grateful for the lessons our relationship teaches us."

Check-In

Today, we celebrate the love we share and the journey we are on together.

Today, this great thing happened in our relationship and we appreciate it because:

_____

_____

_____

_____

Today, this not so great thing happened to us and this is how we handled it:

_____

_____

_____

_____

Today, how did we show love to each other, even in small ways?

_____

_____

_____

_____

Today, what was a challenge we faced, and how did we handle it together?

_____

_____

_____

> "We approach each day as a new opportunity to grow closer."

WEEKLY REFLECTION

DATE:

DID WE HAVE ANY MISCOMMUNICATIONS OR DISAGREEMENTS?

HOW DID WE HANDLE THEM?

WHAT CAN WE DO DIFFERENTLY NEXT TIME?

> "We actively choose to build a future filled with joy and love."

Growth and Improvement

WHAT CAN WE LET GO OF TO MOVE FORWARD?

_____
_____
_____

HOW CAN WE BE MORE AFFECTIONATE DAILY?

_____
_____
_____

WHAT CAN WE DO TO ADD MORE FUN TO OUR RELATIONSHIP?

_____
_____
_____

HOW CAN WE BECOME BETTER AT GIVING EACH OTHER CONSTRUCTIVE FEEDBACK?

_____
_____
_____

"We are a team and together we achieve greatness."

WEEKLY REFLECTION

DATE:

WHAT WAS THE HIGHLIGHT OF OUR WEEK TOGETHER?

DID WE FACE ANY CHALLENGES THIS WEEK?

HOW DID WE HANDLE THEM?

"We nurture our relationship with kindness, care and attention."

....

....

....

....

....

....

....

....

....

....

....

....

OPEN
COMMUNICATION

RESPECT
FOR
BOUNDARIES

TRUST KEYS

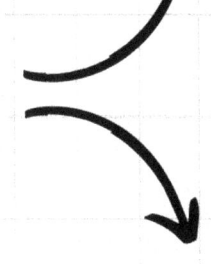

RELIABILITY

DEPENDABILITY

Love Letters

Reflect on a special memory and why it's meaningful to you.

Love Letters

> "We trust the process of growing together and learning from each other."

WEEKLY REFLECTION

DATE:

DID WE HAVE ANY MISCOMMUNICATIONS OR DISAGREEMENTS?

-
-
-

HOW DID WE HANDLE THEM?

-
-
-

WHAT CAN WE DO DIFFERENTLY NEXT TIME?

> "Our love is a space where we both feel heard, valued and respected."

Check-In

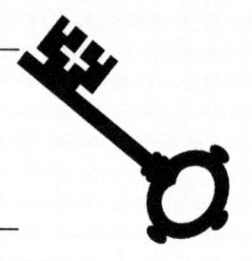

Today, we celebrate the love we share and the journey we are on together.

Today, this great thing happened in our relationship and we appreciate it because:

_____

_____

_____

_____

Today, this not so great thing happened to us and this is how we handled it:

_____

_____

_____

_____

Today, how did we show love to each other, even in small ways?

_____

_____

_____

_____

Today, what was a challenge we faced, and how did we handle it together?

_____

_____

_____

"Together, we explore the beauty of vulnerability and trust."

WEEKLY REFLECTION

DATE:

WHAT WAS THE HIGHLIGHT OF OUR WEEK TOGETHER?

_____

_____

DID WE FACE ANY CHALLENGES THIS WEEK?

- _____
- _____

_____

_____

_____

_____

HOW DID WE HANDLE THEM?

- _____
- _____
- _____

_____

_____

_____

_____

"Together, we create a love that feels like home."

RELATIONSHIP REFLECTION

What's one thing I could improve to make our relationship stronger?

_____
_____
_____
_____
_____

What are some boundaries we could set to improve our relationship?

_____
_____
_____
_____
_____

How do you think we've grown emotionally since being together?

_____
_____
_____
_____
_____

How do you feel about the balance between romance and friendship in our relationship?

_____
_____
_____
_____

What's one thing I could do to make you feel more secure in our relationship?

_____
_____
_____

"We are unstoppable when we stand together in love."

WEEKLY REFLECTION

DATE:

DID WE HAVE ANY MISCOMMUNICATIONS OR DISAGREEMENTS?

-
-
-

HOW DID WE HANDLE THEM?

-
-
-

WHAT CAN WE DO DIFFERENTLY NEXT TIME?

"Together, we create a life
filled with love and adventure."

Check-In

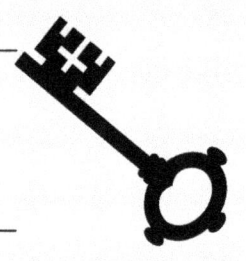

Today, we celebrate the love we share and the journey we are on together.

Today, this great thing happened in our relationship and we appreciate it because:

_____

_____

_____

_____

Today, this not so great thing happened to us and this is how we handled it:

_____

_____

_____

_____

Today, how did we show love to each other, even in small ways?

_____

_____

_____

_____

Today, what was a challenge we faced, and how did we handle it together?

_____

_____

_____

_____

> "Our love is unwavering and we choose loyalty every day."

WEEKLY REFLECTION

DATE:

WHAT WAS THE HIGHLIGHT OF OUR WEEK TOGETHER?

_____

_____

DID WE FACE ANY CHALLENGES THIS WEEK?

- _____
- _____

_____

_____

_____

HOW DID WE HANDLE THEM?

- _____
- _____
- _____

_____

_____

_____

_____

> "We stay committed to each other, honoring our bond with faithfulness."

RELATIONSHIP CHECKLIST
Where are we now?

Place an (X) in the box in your column if you do any
or all of the following.

	His	Hers
Compliment your partner	☐	☐
Listen to your favorite music together	☐	☐
Laugh Together	☐	☐
Plan a weekly date night	☐	☐
Hug, hold hands, or kiss for 10 seconds	☐	☐
Set aside time to talk without distractions	☐	☐
Send a sweet text message	☐	☐
Take a walk together	☐	☐
Spend quality time together	☐	☐

> "Our faithfulness keeps us united, and our love grows stronger over time."

Marriage Keys

1. Regular Check-ins
Set aside time weekly or monthly to check in on your relationship.

2. SHOW APPRECIATION
Regularly express gratitude for the little things.

3. Learn to Compromise
Be willing to compromise on disagreements or preferences to find solutions that work for both of you.

4. Communicate Expectations
Be clear and. honest about your needs, desires, and expectations.

"Our relationship thrives on trust, creating safety and security."

Growth and Improvement

HOW CAN WE SUPPORT EACH OTHER'S EMOTIONAL HEALTH?

_____

_____

_____

WHAT'S SOMETHING WE CAN DO TO IMPROVE OUR FINANCIAL PLANNING AS A TEAM?

_____

_____

_____

HOW CAN WE BUILD HEALTHIER HABITS?

_____

_____

_____

HOW CAN WE CREATE HEALTHIER BOUNDARIES AROUND TECHNOLOGY AND SCREEN TIME?

_____

_____

_____

> "Our hearts are intertwined, and our dreams are aligned."

RELATIONSHIP REFLECTION

What is one thing we've been avoiding discussing and how can we address it?

_____
_____
_____
_____
_____

How do you feel about the way we make important decisions together?

_____
_____
_____
_____
_____

What are your hopes for our relationship in the future?

_____
_____
_____
_____
_____

What is a small thing I can do that makes a big difference in your day?"

_____
_____
_____
_____

What is an adventure or challenge that we have not faced together that you'd like to?

_____
_____
_____

"With love as our guide, every day is a new adventure."

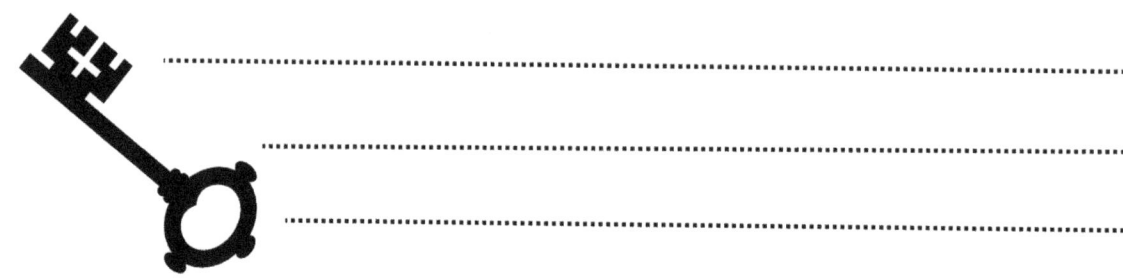

WEEKLY REFLECTION

DATE:

DID WE HAVE ANY MISCOMMUNICATIONS OR DISAGREEMENTS?

-
-
-

HOW DID WE HANDLE THEM?

-
-
-

WHAT CAN WE DO DIFFERENTLY NEXT TIME?

OUR Journal OUR Journey OUR Story

As you reach the final page of this journal, let's take a moment to reflect on the journey you've traveled together. Each entry has been a piece of your story. Take a moment to reflect on the memories you've built and the growth you've experienced.

These pages are a reminder of how far you've come and a testament to the bond you continue to build.

This isn't the end, but a beautiful transition to the next chapter in your lives together. The memories you've captured here will stay with you, reminding you of the love and commitment you share.

As you turn the last page,
keep choosing each other, nurturing your connection, and writing new chapters filled with love, growth, and endless possibilities!

Printed in the USA
CPSIA information can be obtained
at www.ICGtesting.com
CBHW040042271124
18026CB00060B/1479